Words of Life, Words of Hope
Ancient Words will guide you home.
Loretta Sommers #51

Nine Fruits of the Spirit

of the Spirit

Spirit

A Bible Study on Developing Christian Character

Faithfulness

Robert Strand

New Leaf Press

A Division of New Leaf Publishing Group

First printing: June 1999
Third printing: September 2009

Copyright © 1999 by New Leaf Press. All rights reserved. No part
of this book may be used or reproduced in any manner whatsoever
without written permission of the publisher, except in the case of
brief quotations in articles and reviews. For information write:
New Leaf Press, P.O. Box 726, Green Forest, AR 72638.

ISBN-13: 978-0-89221-467-9
ISBN-10: 0-89221-467-8
Library of Congress Number: 99-64012

Cover by Janell Robertson

Printed in China

Please visit our website for other great titles:
www.newleafpress.net

For information regarding author interviews, please contact the
publicity department at (870) 438-5288.

Contents

Introduction

There is an ancient story out of the Middle East which tells of three merchants crossing the desert. They were traveling at night in the darkness to avoid the heat of the day. As they were crossing over a dry creek bed, a loud attention-demanding voice out of the darkness commanded them to stop. They were then ordered to get down off their camels, stoop down and pick up pebbles from the creek bed, and put them into their pockets.

Immediately after doing as they had been commanded, they were then told to leave that place and continue until dawn before they stopped to set up camp. This mysterious voice told them that in the morning they would be both sad and happy. Understandably shaken, they obeyed the voice and traveled on through the rest of the night without stopping. When morning dawned, these three merchants anxiously looked into their pockets. Instead of finding the pebbles as expected, there were precious jewels! And, they were both happy and sad. Happy that they had picked up some of the pebbles, but sad because they hadn't gathered more when they had the opportunity.

This fable expresses how many of us feel about the treasures of God's Word. There is coming a day when we will be thrilled because we have absorbed as much as we have, but sad because we had not gleaned much more. Jewels are best shown off when held up to a bright light and slowly turned so that each polished facet can catch and reflect the light.

Each of these nine jewels of character will be examined in the light of God's Word and how best to allow them to be developed in the individual life. That is how I feel about the following three verses from Paul's writings which challenge us with what their Christian character or personality should look like. Jesus Christ has boiled down a Christian's responsibility to two succinct commands: Love the Lord your God with all your heart, mind, soul, and body, and love your neighbor like yourself. Likewise, Paul the apostle has captured for us the Christian personality in nine traits:

> But the fruit of the Spirit is love, joy, peace, patience, kindness, goodness, faithfulness, gentleness, and self-control. Against such things there is no law. Those who belong to Christ Jesus have crucified the sinful nature with its passions and desires. Since we live by the Spirit, let us keep in step with the Spirit (Gal. 5:22–25).

At the very beginning of this study, I must point out a subtle, yet obvious, distinction. The "fruit" of the Spirit is a composite description of what the Christian lifestyle and character traits are all about — an unbroken whole. We can't pick only the fruit we like.

Unlocked in these nine portraits are the riches of a Christ-centered personality. The thrill of the search is ahead of us!

Faithfulness

PISTOS (Greek), meaning: to be trusted,
reliable, believing, to be counted
on at all times, of a firm persuasion, faithful.

THE FRUIT OF THE
SPIRIT IS... FAITHFULNESS

This seventh fruit of the Spirit is the word for standing fast,
steadfastness, loyal, devoted, tried, constant, reliable, unwavering,
trustworthy, dependable, resolute, honest, punctual, and steady.
Quite a quality of character. This fruit could also be called fidelity.

It also speaks of endurance — a firmness of purpose, especially when the living is tough. It is more than a "grin-and-bear-it" kind of attitude.

It's a very positive, active attribute of character and a much-needed one in today's flippant, irresponsible world. The faithful person is dependable in all kinds of life circumstances. This is a much-desired characteristic in others with whom we have any kind of relationship. We all need to be people of faithfulness!

D.L. Moody said: "I believe in a faith that you can see; a living, working faith that prompts action. Faith without works is like a man putting all his money into the foundation of a house; and works without faith is like building a house on sand without any foundation."

God is the source and standard of faithfulness which He has demonstrated in His dealings with the human race. In the New Testament, Jesus Christ models this same kind of faithfulness in relationships with His followers. The Holy Spirit is ready to bring this trait of character to full maturity in your life and mine . . . so that we, too, can be counted on to be faithful in all circumstances with all our relationships.

It's an old hymn which can usually be found in most any denominational church hymnal. In fact, you may have sung it the last time you were in church and it will do all of us good to contemplate these words as we begin this study:

Great is Thy faithfulness, O God my Father;
There is no shadow of turning with Thee;
Thou changest not, Thy compassions, they fail not;
As Thou hast been, Thou forever wilt be.

Summer and winter and springtime and harvest,
Sun, moon, and stars in their courses above
Join with all nature in manifold witness
To Thy great faithfulness, mercy, and love.

Pardon for sin and a peace that endureth,
Thine own dear presence to cheer and to guide;
Strength for today and bright hope for tomorrow,
Blessings all mine, with ten thousand beside!

(Chorus)
Great is Thy faithfulness! Great is Thy faithfulness!
Morning by morning new mercies I see;
All I have needed Thy hand hath provided;
Great is Thy faithfulness, Lord, unto me!

(Thomas O. Chisholm)

Faith and faithfulness are closely linked — faith being foundational to all that we believe and act upon. Faith is that undefinable power through which we can realize as reality things that are as yet unseen. Faithfulness is the working out of this inner belief system. When we have faith in God, we act in faithful ways. Acts of faithfulness are the demonstration that we have a true faith in God and such acts are the threads holding our belief and behavior system together. As the writer has said, "faith without works is dead."

Let's begin our study with a look at the foundation for faithfulness from the "faith" chapter of the Bible. Please read Hebrews 11:1–40.

Write in your own words the biblical definition of faith:

_____

_____

How are we to apply faith to our daily living?

_____

_____

_____

_____

_____

Which "hero" of the faith do you think was most faithful? Why?

_____

_____

_____

_____

_____

_____

How was it possible for them to believe and never see the fulfillment take place in their lifetime?

_____

_____

_____

_____

_____

How much faith is required in order to be faithful and pleasing to God?

_____

_____

_____

_____

_____

How does God demonstrate that He is faithful in this study?

_____

_____

_____

_____

Can you find any "flawed" people who are listed among these heroes of the faith? List them:

_____

_____

_____

_____

How is it possible to be flawed and still be listed in this chapter?

_____

_____

_____

_____

From verses 32–38, what deductions do you make about faith and how it functions?

_____

_____

_____

_____

How has God's faithfulness been demonstrated even to people who are not perfect?

_____

_____

_____

_____

Explain how God's faithfulness brings hope to all who are so human:

_____

_____

_____

From verse 40, what is the "something better" God planned for us?

_____

_____

_____

_____

_____

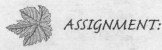 ASSIGNMENT:

• In your own words, write a description of what a "faithful" person would be:

_____

_____

_____

_____

_____

_____

• List the ways in which God has been faithful to you:

_____

_____

_____

_____

_____

WHEN THERE IS NO FAITHFULNESS

Faithfulness is a vital part of the human being . . . in fact it's so important that without it society will collapse. Every day demands from us an act of faith that propels us into countless actions which are dependent on the faithfulness of others. We eat food we haven't prepared or checked out, we fly on airplanes that we trust have been examined faithfully, we trust our health to doctors whose training and background has been adequately prepared, we trust that others will faithfully obey traffic laws, we elect leaders that we hope will be faithful in duty, and on and on we could go. We live by faith and faithfulness because we have been created to live and function in such an environment of trust.

One reason for the lack of faith and faithfulness is that so many of us have been betrayed in our dealings and relationships. Without faithfulness functioning disaster is created. Some have trusted in medicine only to receive cyanide; we have trusted a banker and found out he was a crook; some have trusted a spouse only to discover a hidden alcoholic or adulterer; we have trusted an evangelist to later discover a charlatan. In all of this, there is one positive treasure — GOD IS ALWAYS FAITHFUL! He has no false advertising claims, no broken promises, no deceptive business practices, no chicanery behind the scenes, no spin doctors. GOD IS FAITHFUL! It's the rock of foundation upon which we can build a life!

Are you concerned about faithfulness? Think — IF things were right only 99.9 percent of the time, there would be: one hour of unsafe drinking water every month; two unsafe landings every day at Chicago's O'Hare Airport; 16,000 pieces of lost mail every hour; 20,000 incorrect drug prescriptions every year; 500 incorrect surgeries every week; 50 babies would be dropped on the floor at birth every day; 32,000 heartbeats per person would be missed per year, 22,000 checks would be deducted from the wrong checking account every hour! Now that's only IF things and people were faithful and right 99.9 percent of the time!

What happens when there is a breakdown, when people fail to be faithful to vows and promises? That's the theme of our next study . . . sometimes a study in contrast or the negative gives us insight to the positive.

Let's read from the last of the Old Testament writers, Malachi 2:10–17; 3:13–18.

Have you ever had someone break a commitment made to you? Describe how you felt and how you reacted:

_____

_____

_____

_____

In reading from verses 10–14, specifically, what commitments have been broken by the Israelites?

_____

_____

_____

_____

From verse 10, what happens by "breaking faith" with another?

_____

_____

_____

Is there a connection between God and the faithfulness of His people? Explain:

_____

_____

_____

_____

How does God respond when His people are faithful?

_____

_____

_____

_____

When they are unfaithful?

_____

_____

_____

_____

What are the actions which God specifically hates?

_____

_____

_____

_____

Look at verse 10 . . . what is the point being made by Malachi?

_____

_____

_____

_____

_____

_____

What is the current life lesson which can be learned from verses 11 and 12?

_____

_____

_____

_____

_____

_____

God makes some very specific statements in regard to marriage. List these:

_____

_____

_____

_____

_____

In verse 13, the people seem to be confused about God's reaction. What was their problem?

_____

_____

_____

_____

_____

_____

In Malachi 3:13–18, there are a number of blessings and benefits listed that God will bestow on the faithful. What are they?

_____

_____

_____

_____

From verse 18, specifically, what is the distinction "between those who serve God and those who do not"?

_____

_____

_____

_____

God is faithful. He does not change due to AGE . . . He does not change as to PLACE . . . and He does not change as to HIS WORD.

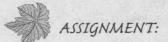 *ASSIGNMENT:*

• List any of your current or past relationships in which lack of faithfulness has played a part:

_____

_____

_____

_____

_____

• In the future, what will you be doing to insure faithfulness on your part in these relationships?

_____

_____

_____

_____

GOD'S PROMISE OF SUPPORT

Have you ever been faced with a task, project, or responsibility that seemed beyond your strength and ability? Something that simply was overwhelming and too massive to deal with alone? Sure, haven't we all at some time been confronted with obstacles we didn't know how to handle?

Stop and think with me about the faithfulness of God and how unchanging He is. He does not change due to AGE . . . even though He is called the Ancient of Days. He does not get older with the passing of time. He is no older today than He was when He breathed the breath of life into Adam so long ago.

God does not change as to PLACE . . . He fills heaven and earth with His presence. He is everywhere! When the Bible speaks of God's visiting earth or that His presence departed, we understand that this does not

Have I not commanded you? Be strong and courageous. Do not be terrified; do not be discouraged, for the Lord your God will be with you wherever you go (Josh. 1:9).

signify as much a change of His location as it denotes a special demonstration of His apparent presence.

God does not change as to His WORD . . . the Bible declares that His Word is forever settled in Heaven. Heaven and earth will pass away, but not His Word! You see, He is marked by total faithfulness and perfection. Now, this is the God who has promised His help and faithfulness to all kinds of people in all kinds of situations.

For our next study, let's see how this worked out in the leadership of one man faced with a massive challenge. Please read Joshua 1:1–9.

How many people will Joshua be leading?

_____

Has there been a time in your life when you were faced with a challenge that seemed too huge to handle by yourself? Explain:

_____

_____

_____

_____

Describe in your own words what you think Joshua must have felt like as this transition was taking place:

_____

_____

_____

_____

_____

_____

What are the promises that God gave to Joshua?

_____

_____

_____

_____

_____

_____

Why were these so encouraging?

_____

_____

_____

_____

_____

In verse 5, God promised, "I will never leave you nor forsake you." Does this stand alone or are there other biblical passages which say much the same thing? If so, please list some of them:

_____

_____

_____

_____

_____

_____

What is God asking of Joshua in order to experience success in his leadership?

_____

_____

_____

_____

_____

_____

Explain what it means to "meditate" on the Book of the Law day and night:

_____

_____

_____

_____

_____

What is there about the Word of God that can help and strengthen us?

_____

_____

_____

_____

_____

Do you think that these promises made to Joshua apply to you and your situation today? Please explain:

_____

_____

_____

_____

_____

How could you go about being "strong and courageous"?

_____

_____

_____

_____

_____

How do the lessons of this passage help you to become bold, strong, and courageous in your daily living?

_____

_____

_____

_____

_____

_____

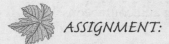

ASSIGNMENT:

• What do these passages say to you and your current situation?

_____

_____

_____

_____

_____

• Think of a friend, family member, or neighbor who needs your support in their current difficult situation. How can you help or encourage that person?

_____

_____

_____

_____

_____

GOD'S PROMISE TO BE THERE

Archaeology has given us any number of insights into the past. One of these snapshots out of the past happened when the city of Pompeii was destroyed by the volcanic eruption of Mt. Vesuvius. When digging through these ancient ruins, archaelogists found many persons buried in some very different positions. Some were found in deep basement vaults where they had run for safety. Others were found in attic chambers where they had hidden themselves from the hot lava flow.

But where did they find the Roman soldier who stood as a sentinel? They found him still standing at the gate of the city where he had been stationed by his captain, with his hands still grasping the weapon, a spear. There, while the earth shook beneath him; there, while the floods of ashes and cinders overwhelmed him, he had stood and not

God has made the promise in many places in the Bible: "I will never leave you, I will never forsake you!"

abandoned his post of duty until he was engulfed by the hot, molten rock. And there he was unearthed after a thousand years.

What a picture of faithfulness, duty, and responsibility!

Faithfulness conveys the concept that someone will be there when we really need them. God has made this promise in any number of places in the word — it's a promise of His which brings comfort to all who might be struggling with life. What a comfort to hear it again, "I will never leave you, I will never forsake you!"

It's in the process that we, too, learn how to become faithful. It's as we handle the little things with consistency, steadiness, and faithfulness that we learn how to be faithful in all things. We may not think anything is happening . . . but God sees the process and He knows what is happening inside of you as you work your way through struggle after struggle. Let's take a moment to consider the process.

A COMMONPLACE LIFE

"A commonplace life," we say, and we sigh;
Yet why should we sigh as we say?
The commonplace sun in the commonplace day.
The moon and the stars, they are commonplace things,

The flower that blooms, and the robin that sings;
Yet sad were the world and unhappy our lot
If flowers all failed and the sunshine came not!
And, GOD, who considers each separate soul,
From commonplace lives makes a beautiful whole.
(Author is unknown)

In our next study, we have God's promise to be there and the wonderful story of two women, Ruth and Naomi. Ruth, the daughter-in-law, makes an astonishing promise — a commitment to be there. Well, enough, let's read our texts: Lamentations 3:19–26; Ruth 1:1–22.

Have you ever been disappointed because someone you had counted on to be there in your need was unfaithful? Explain how that made you feel:

_____

_____

_____

_____

_____

The writer of Lamentations is apparently in a desperate situation. Why does he have hope?

_____

_____

_____

_____

_____

_____

Why is God faithful?

_____

_____

_____

_____

_____

What is to be our response to the faithfulness of God?

_____

_____

_____

Can you think of some ways in which God's faithfulness has been recently demonstrated in your life?

_____

_____

_____

_____

Now, let's go to Ruth 1. Why is faithfulness such an important quality of lasting relationships?

_____

_____

_____

Describe the desperate situation in which Naomi finds herself:

_____

_____

_____

_____

_____

_____

From verses 6–13, what do you discover about Naomi's relationship with God?

_____

_____

_____

_____

_____

_____

Why do you think Naomi encouraged Ruth and Orpah to remain behind in Moab?

_____

_____

_____

_____

_____

In verses 16 and 17, we have the finest declaration of faithfulness, trust, and commitment to be found in or out of biblical literature. What does this passage say to you about faithfulness?

_____

_____

_____

_____

_____

_____

Explain how this action of faithfulness from Ruth must have been a help and encouragement to Naomi:

_____

_____

_____

_____

_____

The bottom line in this story is that eventually, in God's timing, Ruth became part of the lineage of David and in the line of Jesus Christ. What a reward! What do you think will be the ultimate rewards God gives to people who are faithful?

_____

_____

_____

_____

_____

_____

ASSIGNMENT:

• What are some of the life situations in which you think it is important for us to be there?

_____

_____

_____

_____

_____

• Do you have any relationships currently which need your faithfulness to be shown? If so, explain how you will manifest faithfulness:

_____

_____

_____

_____

_____

THE REWARDS OF FAITHFULNESS

Think with me of some of the times when opportunity knocked and no one answered.

WHEN the Beatles auditioned for Decca Recording Co. in 1962, the record execs refused to sign the group because they didn't like their sound. Decca bigwig Dick Rose told Beatles' manager Brian Epstein, "Groups with guitars are on their way out." The group went with EMI and the rest is history.

WHEN in 1975 a low-level Hewlett-Packard engineer named Steve Wozniak shared a dream with his pal, Steve Jobs, to build and sell a personal computer for the masses, the pair tinkered together on their own time to create a compact PC. Their invention was offered to Hewlett-Packard, which turned thumbs-down on the idea. So Wozniak and Jobs went off on their own, founded Apple Computer, Inc. and helped revolutionize the PC industry.

WHAT candy company felt like choking on its own candy after it chose not to allow its product to be used in the film *E.T.*? M & M/Mars . . . the company decided that nothing could be gained by allowing "M & Ms" to appear in the movie. So Elliot wound up luring the lovable alien with "Hershey's Reece's Pieces." That memorable scene would end up luring millions of people into the stores to buy "Reece's Pieces." Thanks to this megahit, Hershey's sales shot up 65 percent!

The following sad commentary was penned by John Greenleaf Whittier in *Maud Muller,* "For all of the sad words of tongue and pen, the saddest of these: it might have been." This is what we are talking about in the parable under study. One of the goals of life for all of us should be to live so that when the final accounting and judgment is completed, we, you, or me will be able to hear, "Well done, good and FAITHFUL servant! You have been faithful with a few things; I will put you in charge of many things. Come and share your Master's happiness!" I can think of nothing more exciting or rewarding than those words!

A "talent" was a measure of weight and money used by the Greeks, much like an ounce or pound is a Western weight term. At the time of Christ, a talent contained 60 "minae" and 6,000 "drachmae." This would have been a huge sum of money in Christ's day.

It's imprecise, but for the sake of understanding, let's use $100,000 as a figure . . . five, two, and one talents . . . $500,000, $200,000, and $100,000.

One more thing to understand — this money didn't belong to any of these servants, it was always the Master's, but it was to be invested, used, and accounted for. It was not a gift.

Each of us have been placed on earth as a caretaker of God's business. We have been given a portion of life and charged with the responsibility of taking care of it, increasing it, investing it, and presenting it back to God.

Jesus tells this parable during the final week of His life on this earth . . . it's almost as if it were a last will and testament. In the same biblical chapter there are two other powerful parables. These three deal with responsibility, accountability, separation, judgment, faithfulness, and a returning Master who will be our judge.

Let's get into our text — Matthew 24:14–30.

To whom is Jesus speaking this parable?

_____

_____

_____

_____

What is the Master expecting of these servants?

_____

_____

_____

_____

Is He still expecting the same things from us, today?

_____

_____

_____

Perhaps this is the point at which we should take an inventory. What are some of the resources, abilities, or talents which have been given to you?

_____

_____

_____

_____

_____

_____

_____

For what are the "faithful" servants rewarded?

_____

_____

_____

_____

_____

For what is the "unfaithful" servant punished?

_____

_____

_____

_____

_____

_____

_____

What specifically makes the third servant "wicked"?

_____

_____

_____

_____

_____

_____

Why do you think the third servant hid the money instead of investing the Master's money?

_____

_____

_____

_____

_____

_____

Does the third servant have a faulty picture of the Master? If you think so, please explain:

_____

_____

_____

_____

_____

_____

Do you think that the "reward" and "punishment" were justly administered? Explain your answer:

_____

_____

_____

_____

_____

Do you think that the Master will be requiring the same kinds of results from us on judgment day?

_____

_____

_____

_____

_____

What kinds of investments are you making with your lifestyle?

_____

_____

_____

_____

_____

 ASSIGNMENT:

• How can the principles of this parable be applied to your relationships today?

_____

_____

_____

_____

_____

• Why is "faithfulness" such an important part of the Christian lifestyle?

_____

_____

_____

_____

_____

IN SUMMARY

EVERYTHING we have is a God-given trust! Everything! Most of us are just average kind of folks, not spectacular, but we can all be faithful. So the bottom-line question is: WHAT HAVE YOU DONE WITH WHAT YOU HAVE BEEN GIVEN? Everybody has been blessed with something . . . everybody! It's not the gift that matters so much, it's how you use the gift you have been given.

Carrying out the garbage is not my gift. But I have to do it, now more than ever, because our kids are grown and gone from home. When they were home I commanded them to do it . . . but they protested that this was not one of their gifts, either. Now I do

WHAT

HAVE

YOU DONE

WITH

WHAT

YOU

HAVE

BEEN

GIVEN?

it so that we are not overwhelmed and buried in garbage.

But I know a man who stops by his invalid neighbor's house three times a week just to empty his garbage. To him, it's a great joy of life, fulfilling this gift, taking out a helpless neighbor's garbage.

No one is equal in talents, but all of us can be equal in our efforts to use our talents. And you will not receive more until you have put to use what has been given to you. What was the reward for doubling the five talents to ten? More responsibility, more talents to care for. The same held true for the two into four. The principle underlying this parable is that God wants you to become a pipeline of His riches and blessings to others, not that you become a purse for yourself.

The unfaithful servant was called "wicked" five times by Jesus. It's a harsh word of condemnation. Why this kind of punishment? Because he wouldn't try. Because fear was the dominant factor of his living. I believe that if he would have tried and lost it, God would have blessed him.

It comes down to a "use-it-or-lose-it" all, including your life. It's as simple and straightforward as any wake-up message could be. This manager was lazy and fearful, which in turn led to Christ calling him "wicked."

Henry Van Dyke wrote: "The woods would be silent if no birds sang except those that sang the best."

Here's the universal life-principle dealing with faithfulness: IF YOU HAVE A GIFT OR TALENT AND YOU USE IT FAITHFULLY, GOD INCREASES IT SO YOU CAN DO EVEN MORE. If you have a talent and refuse to use it, you lose it.

This is true of tennis, golf, singing, skiing, writing, piano playing, or even thinking. The only way to keep what you have and increase it is to faithfully invest it in others and for the kingdom of God. Always at work is this law of "accumulative abundance": "For everyone who has will be given more, and he will have an abundance. Whoever does not have, even what he has will be taken from him" (Matt. 25:29).

FAITHFULNESS, as nurtured by the Holy Spirit in your life, is an absolute necessity for productive Christian living! It's a hard, harsh truth. It seems to be a negative until you look at the other side, the positive side. Think with me of the most joyful people you know. . . . Quick, what is their secret of joy? The most joyous people I know are the ones who never stop growing. When you give you get more to give. When you have an increase you have more to increase. When you use it faithfully, you get more to use! In short: Use it faithfully or lose it!

Kenneth Dodge of San Leandro, California, tells this story: In a small town in the Midwest, where I spent six years of my early youth, there lived a mentally challenged adult named Myron. It was during depression years and there was no place for Myron to be kept but at home. He lived with his mother and they managed to survive on the work he did as a gardener. Myron had the proverbial "green thumb" and the places where he did the gardening were easy to identify. The lawns, shrubs, hedges, and flowers all showed loving care, skill, and attention. Myron also did "volunteer" work. He cut grass, raked leaves, and planted flowers in what were unsightly vacant lots and for widows and others who couldn't do yard work.

He was probably best known for his oil can. He always carried a small can of lubricating oil in his hip pocket. A squeaky door or hinge or wheel or gate always got a free dose from Myron's oil can.

Never a Sunday went by that Myron was not in church with his mother. Yes, we boys tried to tease him. He always got the better of us because he refused to be anything but cheerful.

Myron died a few years after I left to go to college. It was not easy to arrange, but I went back for his funeral. I was not prepared for what I saw. It seemed that everyone in the town decided to attend the funeral.

Myron had not achieved fame, fortune, or honor. But he had been a worker, an optimist, and most of all—FAITHFUL! He was a man who had made use of the meager gifts given to him. He had patterned for all of us the kind of faithful life that really matters.

The greatest commendation any human being could have bestowed upon him or her would be to hear the Master say:

Let love and faithfulness never leave you; bind them around your neck, write them on the tablet of your heart (Prov. 3:3).

Well done, good and FAITHFUL servant! You have been faithful with a few things; I will put you in charge of many things. COME AND SHARE YOUR MASTER'S HAPPINESS!"

The psalmist Ethan, has the final word:

I will sing of the Lord's great love forever; with my mouth I will make your faithfulness known through all generations. I will declare that your love stands firm forever, that you established your faithfulness in heaven itself (Ps. 89:1–2).

And the fruit of the Spirit is . . . FAITHFULNESS!

Nine Fruits of the Spirit

Study Series includes

Love

Joy

Peace

Patience

Kindness

Goodness

Faithfulness

Gentleness

Self-Control

Robert Strand

Retired from a 40-year ministry career with the Assemblies of God, this "pastor's pastor" is adding to his reputation as a prolific author. The creator of the fabulously successful Moments to Give series (over one million in print), Strand travels extensively, gathering research for his books and mentoring pastors. He and his wife, Donna, live in Springfield, Missouri. They have four children.

Rev. Strand is a graduate of North Central Bible College with a degree in theology.